THERE'S A DIPLODOCUS AT THE DOOR

Aleksei Bitskoff & Ruth Symons

NEW
BURLINGTON
BOOKS

Diplodocus was a giant plant-eating dinosaur

A NEW BURLINGTON BOOK
The Old Brewery
6 Blundell Street
London N7 9BH

Design: Duck Egg Blue
Managing Editor: Victoria Garrard
Design Manager: Anna Lubecka
Dinosaur Expert: Chris Jarvis

Copyright © QED Publishing 2013

First published in the UK in 2013 by
QED Publishing
A Quarto Group company
230 City Road
London EC1V 2TT

www.qed-publishing.co.uk

A catalogue record for this book is available from the British Library.

ISBN 978 1 78171 365 5

Printed in China

with a super-long neck and tail!

He lived around

150 million

years ago – many millions of years before the first humans appeared.

But just imagine if Diplodocus was alive today!

How would he cope with modern life?

What if Diplodocus went to a restaurant?

Diplodocus was a vegetarian so he would order a big plate of salad.

But with his...

looooooooooooooooooooo

ong neck...

Diplodocus could reach all the other tables. He could eat everything in sight without even moving his feet.

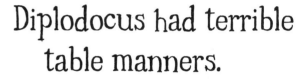

Diplodocus had terrible table manners. He never chewed his food – he just swallowed leaves whole!

What if Diplodocus had a tummy ache?

He might gobble up some stones to make him feel better.

Lots of plant-eating dinosaurs swallowed stones.

That's because they didn't **chew** their food!

Instead, stones inside their tummies helped to **grind up** the leaves they ate.

What if Diplodocus needed a shower?

Diplodocus wouldn't fit in your shower.
But he might just fit in a car wash.

Diplodocus was 27 metres long.

That's the length of three buses!

What if Diplodocus used my loo?

One diplodocus poo would fill up the...

Whole toilet!

Ask him to go in
the garden instead.
Diplodocus poo was full
of nutrients that would
help the plants to grow.

What if Diplodocus lived in the garden?

He'd eat all of the plants – even the prickly ones.

So watch out for your mum's **prize rose!**

But he'd help collect leaves in autumn.
His peggy teeth would act just like a rake.

What if Diplodocus went to the zoo?

He'd be the **biggest** and **heaviest** of all the animals.

Diplodocus's neck was three times longer than a giraffe's – that's 6 metres long!

Diplodocus weighed twice as much as the largest elephant – that's 12 tonnes!

A zebra is just half the height of Diplodocus –
but their heads are the same size!

What if Diplodocus went to a firework display?

Diplodocus wouldn't worry about the noise. He could be just as loud himself.

When he...

cracks

his tail like a whip, it can be heard 10 kilometres away!

Diplodocus used this noise to scare away predators. But he was too big for most dinosaurs to attack anyway.

What if Diplodocus had a birthday party?

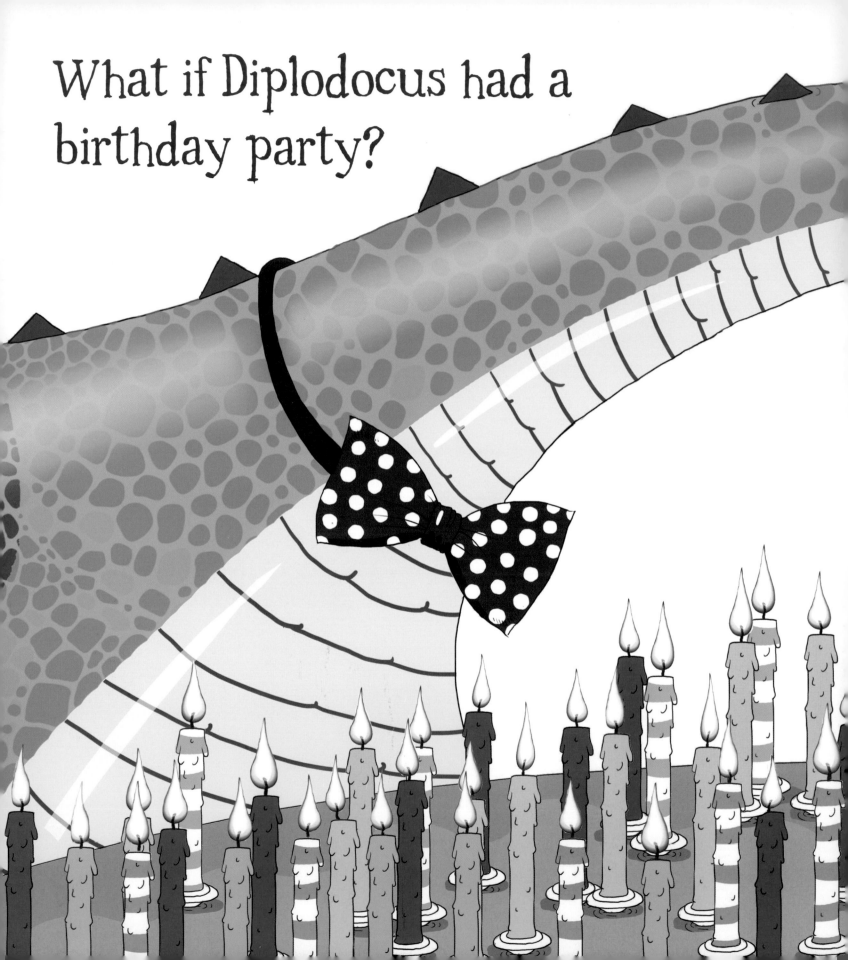

Diplodocus could live to be
100 years old.
That's a lot of candles to blow out!

What if Diplodocus needed a job?

Diplodocus would be very useful on a building site. If he reared up on his hind legs he could reach almost

10 metres up.

That's about three storeys high!

Diplodocus's skeleton

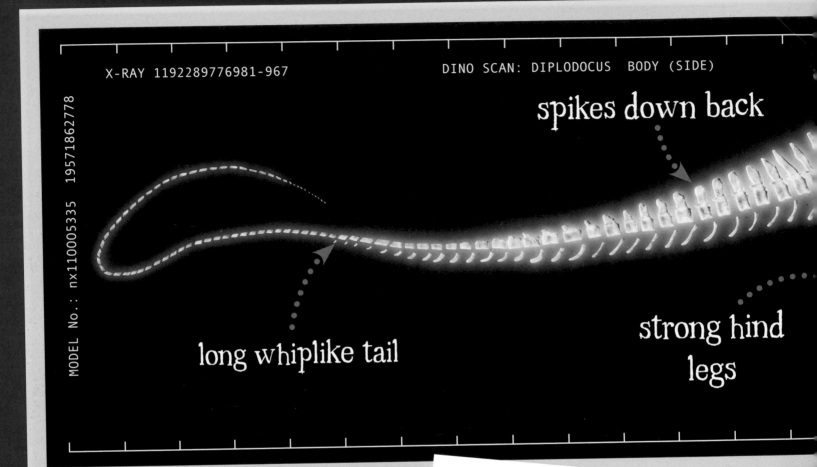

X-RAY 1192289776981-967

DINO SCAN: DIPLODOCUS   BODY (SIDE)

MODEL No.: nx110005335   19571862778

spikes down back

long whiplike tail

strong hind legs

Everything we know about Diplodocus comes from fossils – skeletons that have been in the ground for thousands and thousands of years.

Scientists can look at fossils to work out how dinosaurs lived in the past.

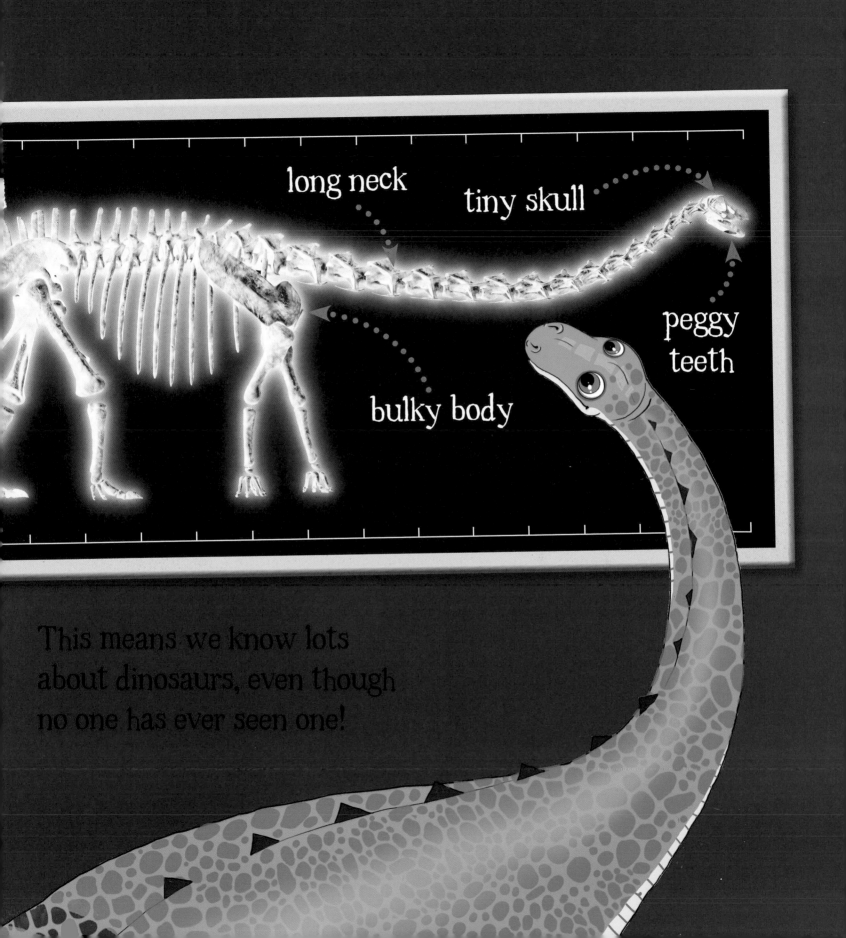

long neck

tiny skull

peggy teeth

bulky body

This means we know lots about dinosaurs, even though no one has ever seen one!

COLORADO, USA
First fossil skeleton discovered – 1878

WYOMING, USA
Fossilized skin found – 1994

WYOMING, USA
Partial skeleton found – 1902

WYOMING, USA
A near-complete young Diplodocus discovered, nicknamed 'Twinky' – 2011

UTAH, USA
Shin bone discovered – 2007

PASSPORT

Diplodocus
(DIP-LO-DO-KUS)

NAME MEANS 'DOUBLE BEAM' THIS REFERS TO THE SHAPE OF BONES IN THE TAIL.

WEIGHT 12–15 TONNES

LENGTH 27 METRES

HEIGHT 3 METRES TO THE SHOULDER

HABITAT WOODS, FOREST

DIET FERNS, LEAVES, PINE NEEDLES

134876357634127632320

D<DIP<<DIPLODOCUS<<<<<<<<<<<<<<3400372543479934<<<<<<<<<<<<<<<<7152622910816546>>>>>>>>